SCHOOL

100 YEARS AGO

by Allison Lassieur

amicus readers 2

amicus readers

Say hello to amicus readers.

You'll find our helpful dog, Amicus, chasing a ball—to let you know the reading level of a book.

(A)

(1)

(2)

Learn to Read

Frequent repetition of sentence structures, high frequency words, and familiar topics provide ample support for brand new readers. Approximately 100 words.

Read Independently

Repetition is mixed with varied sentence structures and 6 to 8 content words per book are introduced with photo label and picture glossary supports. Approximately 150 words.

Read to Know More

These books feature a higher text load with additional nonfiction features such as more photos, time lines, and text divided into sections. Approximately 250 words.

Amicus Readers are published by Amicus
P.O. Box 1329, Mankato, Minnesota 56002
www.amicuspublishing.us

U.S. publication copyright © 2012 Amicus.
International copyright reserved in all countries.
No part of this book may be reproduced in any
form without written permission from the publisher.

Printed in the United States of America at Corporate
Graphics, in North Mankato, Minnesota.

Series Editor   Rebecca Glaser
Series Designer   Heather Dreisbach
Photo Researcher   Heather Dreisbach

Library of Congress Cataloging-in-Publication Data
Lassieur, Allison.
  School: 100 years ago / by Allison Lassieur.
    p. cm. – (Amicus Readers. 100 years ago)
  Includes index.
  Summary: "Discusses turn-of-the-century American schools
  and how they are different from the early 1900s to today.
  Includes "What's Different?" photo quiz"–Provided by
  publisher.
  ISBN 978-1-60753-164-7 (library binding)
  1. Public schools–United States–History–20th century–
  Juvenile literature. I. Title. II. Title: School one hundred
  years ago.
  LA216.L37 2012
  370.973'09041–dc22
                                              2010049883

Photo Credits

Susan Montgomery/Shutterstock, cover; Library of Congress, Prints & Photographs Division, National Child Labor Committee Collection, LC-DIG-nclc-04343, 1, 16, 21m; Western History/Genealogy Dept., Denver Public Library, 4; Library of Congress, Prints & Photographs Division, Detroit Publishing Company Collection, LC-DIG-ppmsca-13304 , 5; Alvin Langdon Coburn/George Eastman House/Getty Images, 6; Library of Congress, Prints & Photographs Division, National Child Labor Committee Collection, LC-DIG-nclc-04357, 7, 20b; Minnesota Reflections/Photographer: Eugene S. Hill (1856-1936) , 9; Buyenlarge/Getty Images, 10, 22t; Image courtesy of the St. Cloud State University Archives, 11, 17, 20m; Michael Siluk/Photolibrary, 13; Minnesota Historical Society/George A. Kamrath, 14, 20t; Library of Congress Prints and Photographs Division Washington, LC-USZ62-135334, 18; Dominik Pabis/iStockphoto, 21t; Library of Congress Prints and Photographs Division Washington, LC-DIG-npcc-00292, 21b; Erik Isakson/Getty Images, 22b

1024   3-2011
10 9 8 7 6 5 4 3 2 1

TABLE OF CONTENTS

Country Schools

One hundred years ago, most children lived in small towns. They went to country schools. Most students walked to school. A few rode buses pulled by horses.

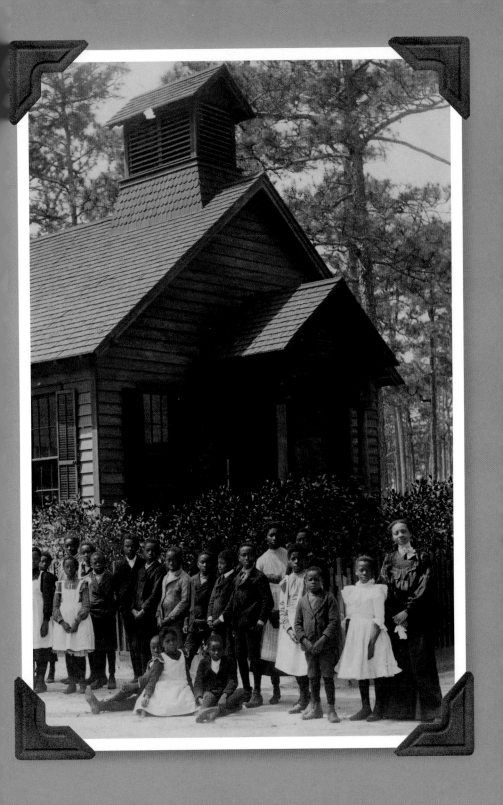

Only about 20 students went to a country school. Country schools had one room. One teacher taught kids of all ages. Light came from the windows. Everyone went to the bathroom outside, in an outhouse.

OUTHOUSE

City Schools

Big cities had larger schools with several stories. Hundreds of students might go to one city school. Most city students lived close to their neighborhood school. They walked to school.

City schools had many classrooms, a gym, and sometimes a library. One teacher taught each grade. Many city schools had indoor plumbing and electricity.

A Day at School

One hundred years ago, classrooms were quite bare. Desks were usually placed in straight rows and bolted to the floor. Sometimes two students shared one desk. The biggest thing in the classroom was the wood stove. It kept the students warm in winter.

Most schools didn't have cafeterias. Students brought lunch. They ate outside or at their desks. A few schools tried a new idea. They began serving lunch to students. Students could choose soup, stew, bread, or sandwiches. Lunch cost only one penny.

Students learned to read from small books called primers. Sometimes there weren't enough books for everyone. So students recited their lessons out loud.

Teachers wrote on chalkboards, so there was a lot of chalk dust. Everyone wrote their lessons with a pencil and paper. No one had computers or printers.

Most country schools had only a sand pit and a few swings on the playground. City schools sometimes had big playgrounds with swings, seesaws, a sand pit, and basketball hoops. Just like today, recess was the best part of the school day!

PHOTO GLOSSARY

cafeteria—a room where food is served

chalkboard—a hard, smooth slate surface on which chalk is used

outhouse—an outdoor bathroom with no plumbing

plumbing—pipes that bring water into a building and also drain it out

primer—a small book used to teach children to read

recess—a break from school when children can play

WHAT'S DIFFERENT?

How many differences can you spot between
the 1910 classroom and the 2010 classroom?

Ideas for Parents and Teachers

100 Years Ago, an Amicus Readers Level 2 series, introduces children to everyday life around 100 years ago, in the early 1900s. Use the following strategies to help readers predict and comprehend the text.

Before Reading
- Ask the child about school.
- Have him or her describe an ordinary day in the classroom.
- Ask about the objects that the teacher uses to teach, such as books, a chalkboard, and computers.

Read the Book
- Read the book to the child, or have him or her read it independently.
- Point out details in the photos that are interesting or relevant to the child's school day.
- Show the child how to interpret the photos and how the images relate to the text.

After Reading
- Have the child explain the similarities and differences between school life one hundred years ago and today.
- Encourage the child to think further by asking questions such as, *How do you think it would feel to go to school then? What do you think your school day would be like?*

23

I

WEB SITES

School: The Story of American Public Education
http://www.pbs.org/kcet/publicschool/

School Then and Now
http://www.galileo.org/schools/millarville/our-school/important_index.html